Level 2
Becoming a Reader

Book 1: Focusing on learning three-letter "a" words

Amanda Riccetti
Illustrations by Steven Gomez

Library of Congress Control Number: 2019906488
Published in the United States by Kindle Direct Publishing,
an Amazon Company, Seattle, WA.
www.kdp.amazon.com
www.readingwithmissamanda.com

Big City Publishing is a registered trademark of Big City Montessori School.
Library of Congress Cataloging-in-Publication Data

Riccetti, Amanda, 2019–
Reading with Miss Amanda, Level 2: Becoming a Reader—Book 1: Focusing on learning three-letter "a" words
by Amanda Riccetti; Illustrations by Steven Gomez, Design by Robert Riccetti
p.cm.
Summary: In the Level 2 Orange series, Miss Amanda teaches blending letters to read words using the Movable Alphabet lessons.
ISBN-13: 978-1-950675-05-0 | ISBN-10: 1-950675-05-X

Printed in the United States of America

This book is dedicated to every child who wants to learn how to read and the adult in their life who wants to support them.

Contents

What to Expect

PHONETIC LEARNING: Throughout this series, children learn letter sound recognition. In the Montessori Method, we do not call letters "ABC" but rather refer to their sound. Use the phonetic letter sounds listed below to become familiar with the way the sounds will be written throughout the books. Remember to always call letters by their sounds.

PHONETIC LETTER SOUNDS: a- ah, b- buh, c- ck, d- duh, e- eh, f- Fff, g- guh, h- Hhh, i- ih, j- juh, k- ck, l- Lll, m- Mmm, n- Nnn, o- oh, p- /p/, q- kwa, r- Rrr, s- Sss, t- /t/, u- uh, v- Vvv, w- wuh, x- ks, y- yuh, z- Zzz

INTUITIVE LESSONS: The lessons in the *Reading with Miss Amanda* series will feel completely intuitive to children, even if they have different styles of learning. The illustrations and games help to engage younger children at the beginning, then evolve into appealing exercises that will teach your child to read.

TIME SPENT: Expect to spend about 10-20 minutes per day on the book for five days a week. Each book could take as little as one week to master or up to two months, depending on the pace of the child and the level the child is on.

REPETITION IS GOOD: Children love repetition, and it drives learning. For example, the popular book *Goodnight Moon* by Margaret Wise Brown might bore an adult, but children love the repetition of phrases. So if you use this book and think, "that's repetitive," remember — it is designed that way.

Reading with Miss Amanda

5 levels

Level	Typical Age*	Reading Level**	Example
L 1	3+ Pre-Reader	Has not learned letter sounds yet	"ah," "buh," "ck"
L 2	4+ Becoming a Reader	Has not learned to phonetically read three-letter words yet	"Max," "rat," "cat"
L 3	4+ Beginning Reader	Has not learned to read short sentences yet	"The crab ran and hid."
L 4	4+ Budding Reader	Has not learned to read four or five-letter words in short sentences yet	"The crab ran on the sand."
L 5	5+ Advanced Reader	Has not learned silent vowels (cake) or blended vowels (oo, ai) yet	"The cook baked a cake."

*The ages listed are merely guidelines that Montessori teachers use as a basis to introduce reading lessons.

**This series is also ideal for older children who need to learn reading or children with a learning difference, such as dyslexia.

If you have any issues, go to the FAQs at the end of the book.

Hi there! Welcome back to my class! In this book, you will find lessons that will help you learn to read. Practice makes permanent.
Come join me!
a

a
a
cat
rat
Max
ai
snail
abcdefg
hijklm
nopqrst
uvwxyz
rat
bat
mat
ca

Lesson 1

Identifying Letters

Tip

This lesson will familiarize your child with the Movable Alphabet by having them find some familiar letters and letters that may be new to them. The Movable Alphabet provides the bridge to make the connection from letter sounds into words; it is a critical step that must not be skipped or rushed.

During the lesson, watch for signs of readiness, and follow your child's interest as you go through each lesson. There is absolutely no rush, and your child will learn when they are interested and ready. As they go through the lesson, help your child locate the letters if they can't find them easily. Through the repetition, your child will learn the letters.

For this lesson, I will ask you to find some letters from the alphabet. Some you already know and some will be new. Ask for help if you can't locate a letter.

How to do Lesson 1

Follow these steps and learn how:

Step 1: Cover the letters.

Step 2: Read the dialogue by the picture.

Step 3: Move your hand down to reveal each letter after your child finds it. If your child struggles, help them find the letter.

Step 4: Read the text, "Say..."

Please say "try again" if your child chooses the incorrect letter. After two tries, help your child find the letter. You and your child are now ready to practice identifying letters.

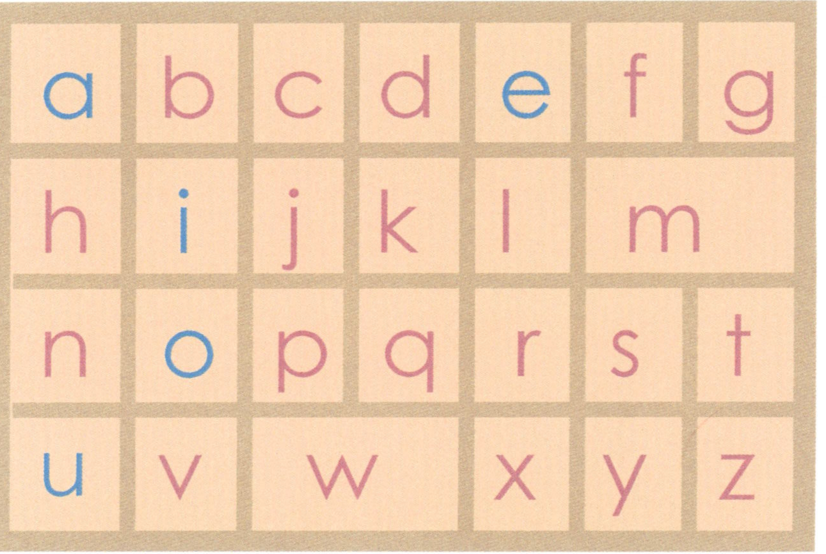

Look at the letterbox.
Please find the letter "Rrr."

Say "Rrr" for "ram."

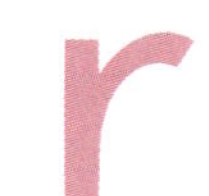

Can you find "Mmm"?

Say "Mmm" for "man."

Can you find "ah"?

Say "ah" for "apple."

Can you find "buh"?

Say "buh" for "bag."

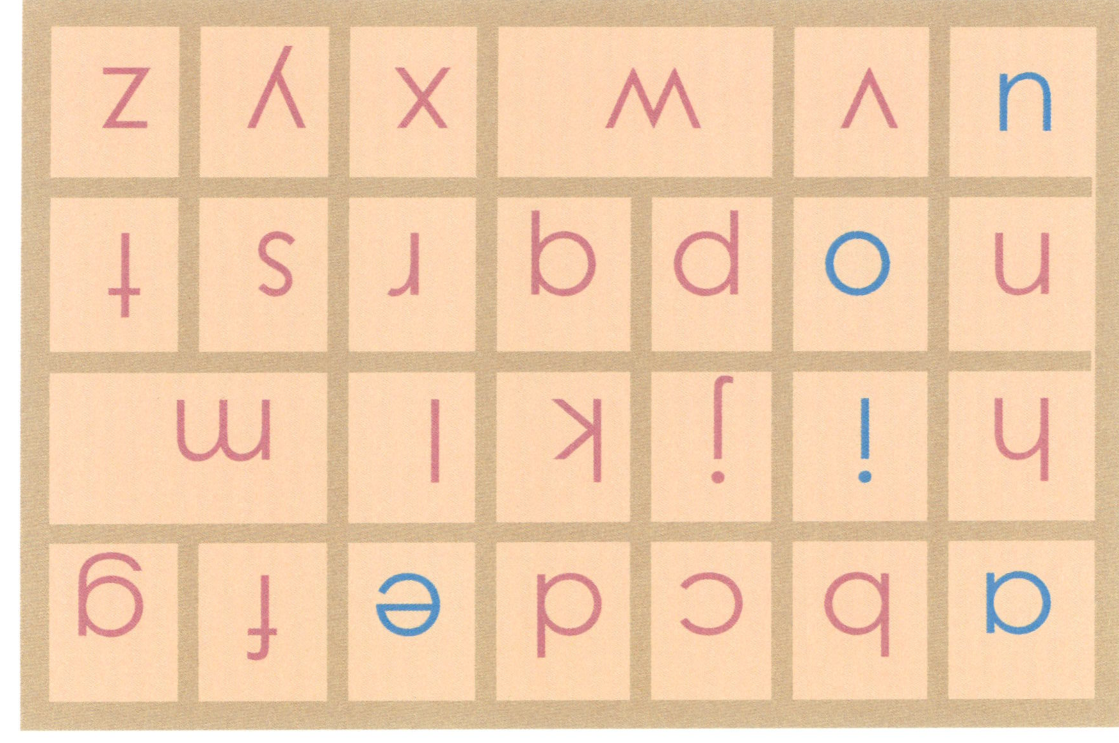
a
b
c
d
e
f
g
h
i
j
k
l
m
n
o
p
q
r
s
t
u
v
w
x
y
z

Look at the letterbox.
Please find the letter "Rrr."

Say "Rrr" for "ram."

r

Can you find "Mmm"?

Say "Mmm" for "man."

Can you find "ah"?

Say "ah" for "apple."

a

Can you find "buh"?

Say "buh" for "bag."

b

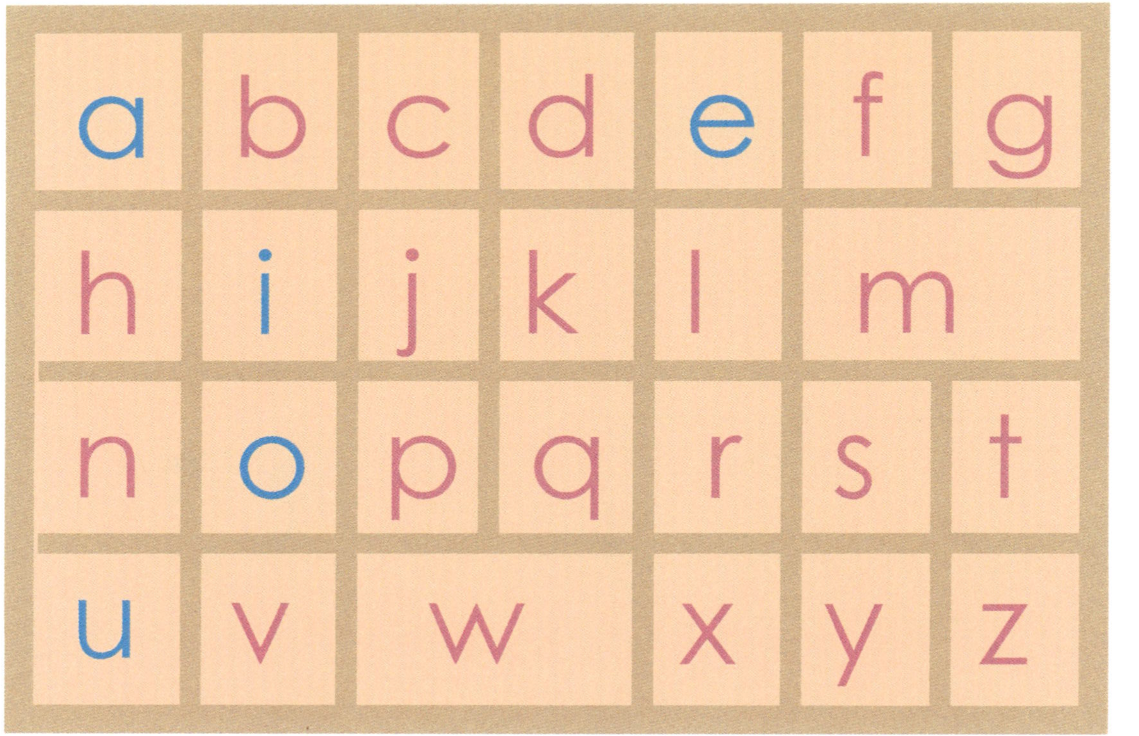
a b c d e f g
h i j k l m
n o p q r s t
u v w x y z

Look at the letterbox.
Please find the letter "ks."

Say "ks" for "ax."

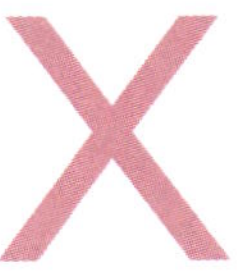

Can you find "Fff"?

Say "Fff" for "fan."

Can you find "guh"?

Say "guh" for "gap."

Can you find "juh"?

Say "juh" for "jam."

j

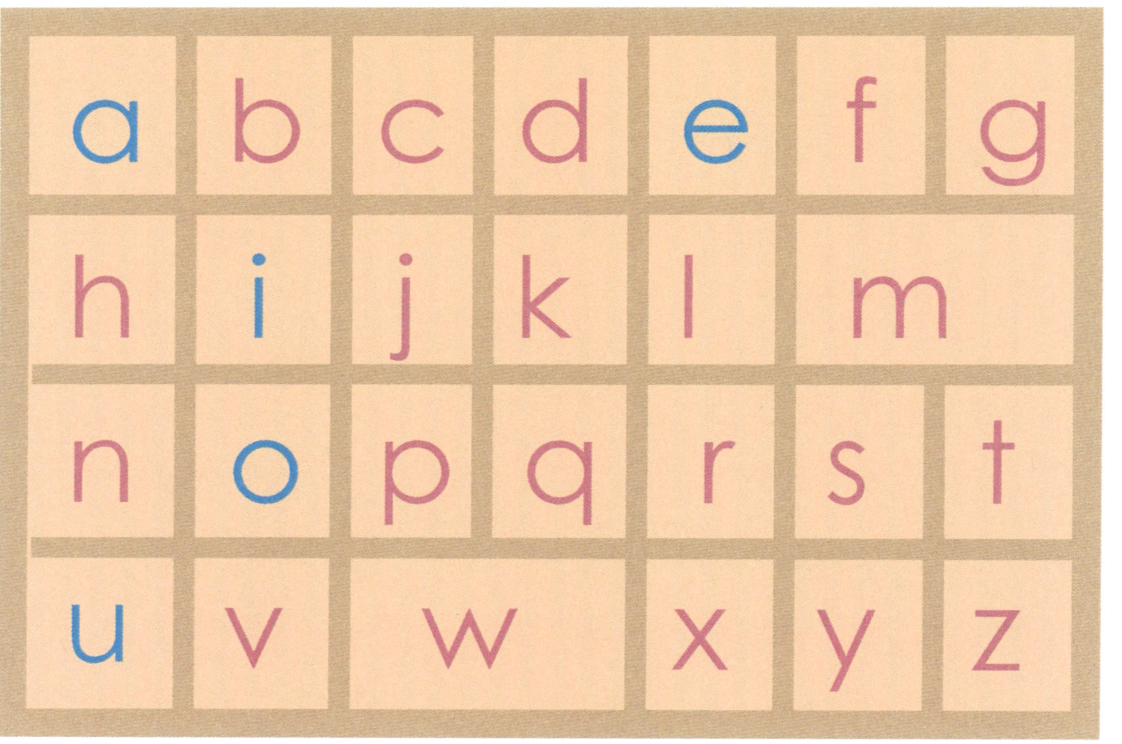
a b c d e f g
h i j k l m
n o p q r s t
u v w x y z

Look at the letterbox.
Please find the letter "wuh."

Say "wuh" for "wax."

Can you find "Nnn"?

Say "Nnn" for "nap."

n

Can you find "yuh"?

Say "yuh" for "yak."

y

Can you find "Vvv"?

Say "Vvv" for "van."

Lesson 2

Matching Letters to Pictures

Tip

This lesson will familiarize your child with the beginning sounds of words. Remember that you can stop at the end of any lesson and can repeat or restart a lesson at any time. Just follow your child's natural pace!

This lesson should be repeated until it's easy for your child. Then, move to the next lesson.

Extension Lesson

Have your child copy the letters they matched and draw a picture to go with them. Then review all the letter sounds.

For this lesson, match a letter to the beginning sound of each picture.
When you point to the correct letter, the letter will be revealed.

How to do Lesson 2

Follow these steps and learn how:

Step 1: Cover the whole letter on the right and read the dialogue above the picture.

Step 2: Reveal the letter after your child finds the correct one. If your child struggles, help them find the letter.

Step 3: Read the text below the picture.

Please say "try again" if your child chooses the incorrect letter. After two tries, help your child find the letter. You and your child are now ready to match letters to pictures.

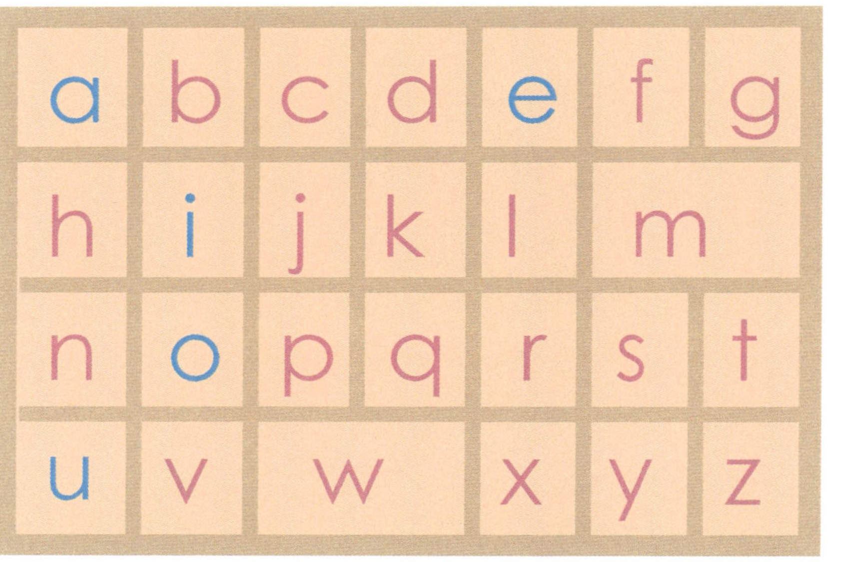

Look at the letterbox.

Please find the letter "buh" for "ball."

Say "buh" for "ball."

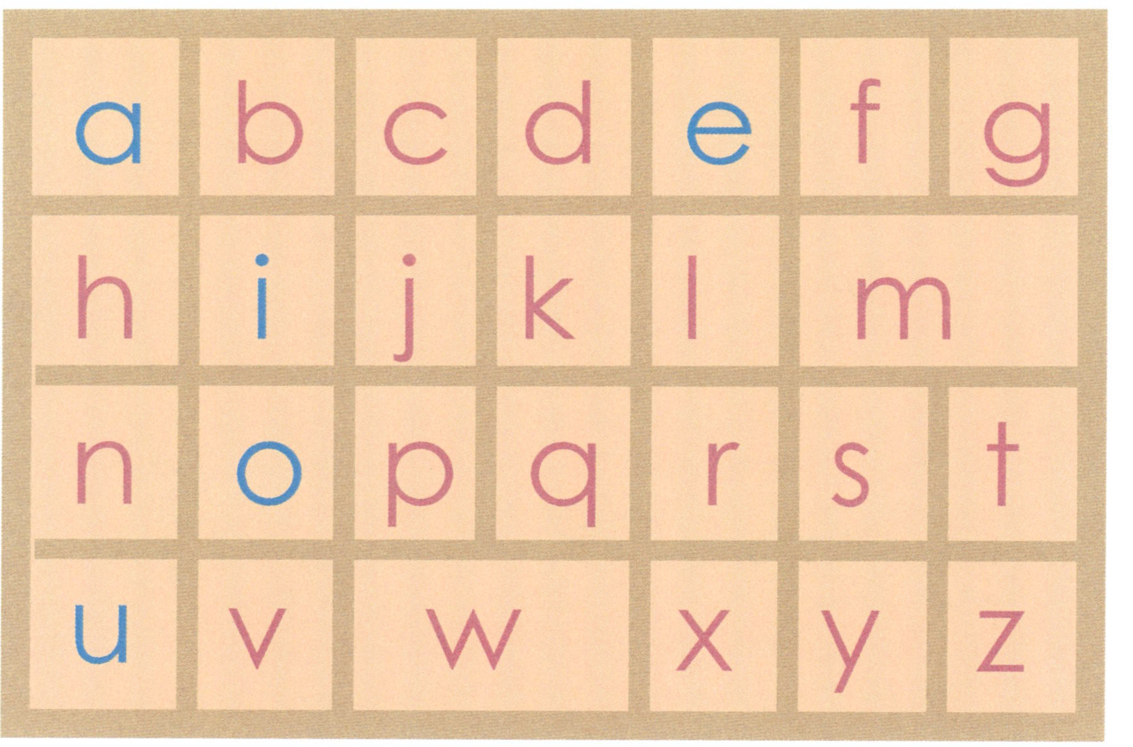

a b c d e f g
h i j k l m
n o p q r s t
u v w x y z

Look at the letterbox.

Please find the letter “buh” for “ball.”

Say “buh” for “ball.”

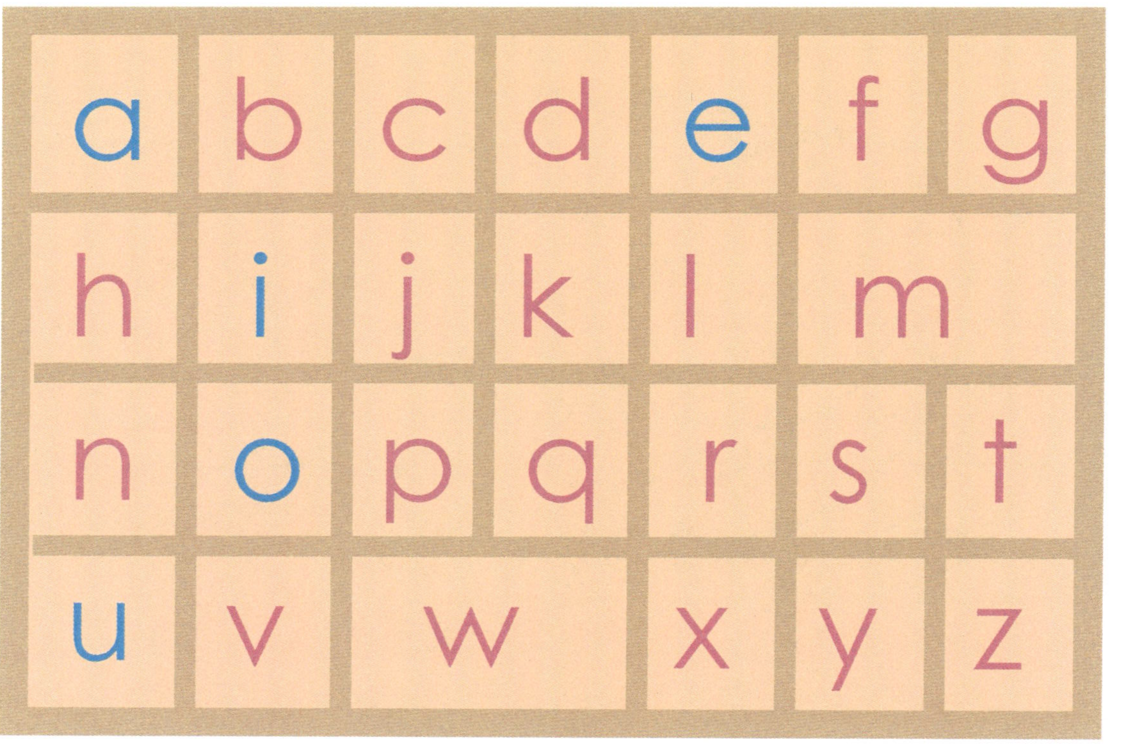
a b c d e f g
h i j k l m
n o p q r s t
u v w x y z

Can you find "ah" for "apple"?

Say "ah" for "apple."

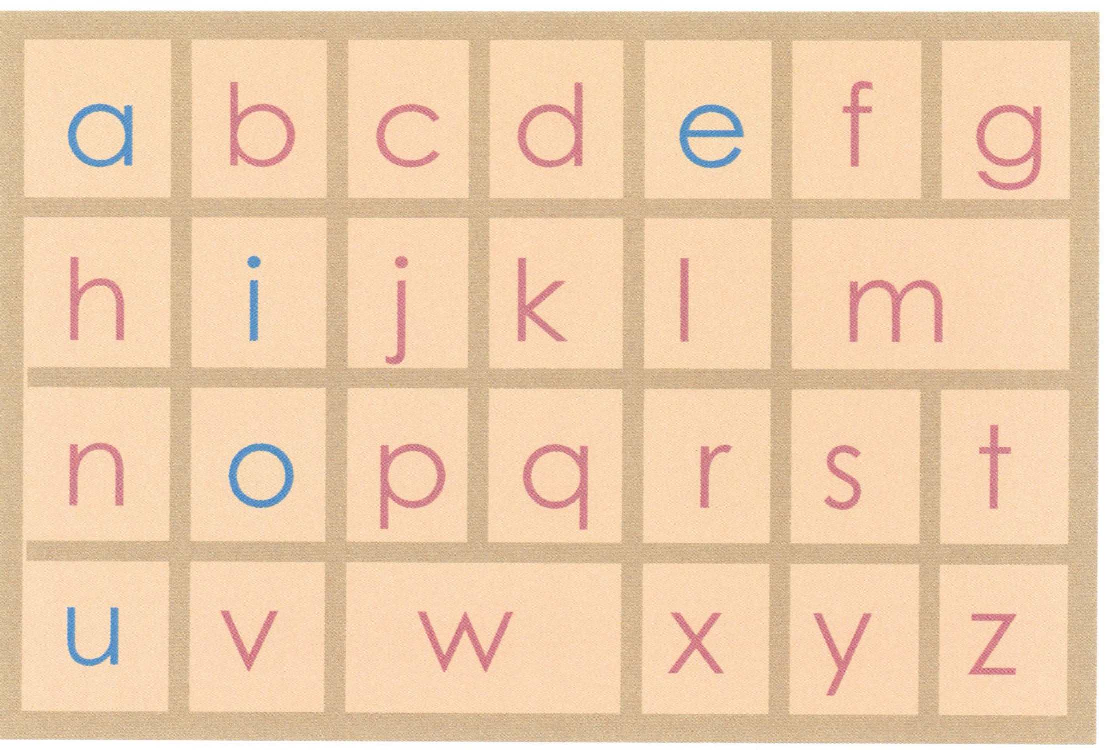
a b c d e f g
h i j k l m
n o p q r s t
u v w x y z

Can you find "/t/" for "turtle"?

t

Say "/t/" for "turtle."

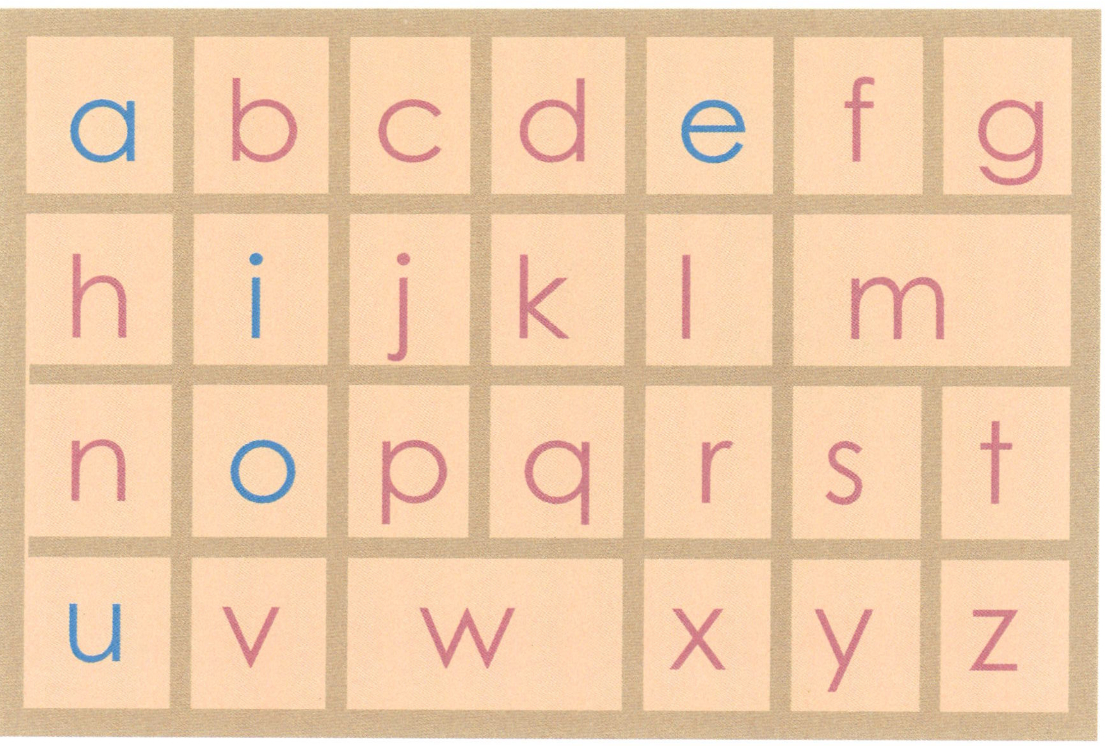
a b c d e f g
h i j k l m
n o p q r s t
u v w x y z

Can you find “Vvv” for “violin”?

V

Say “Vvv” for “violin.”

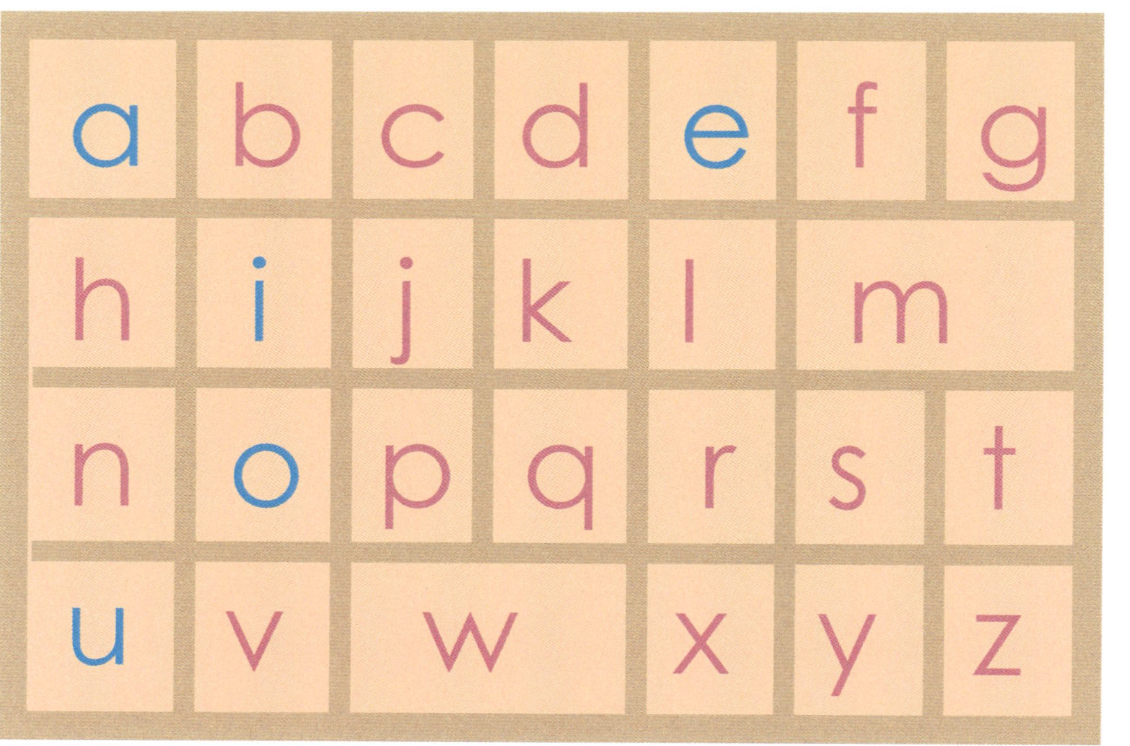
a b c d e f g
h i j k l m
n o p q r s t
u v w x y z

Can you find "ck" for "cat"?

Say "ck" for "cat."

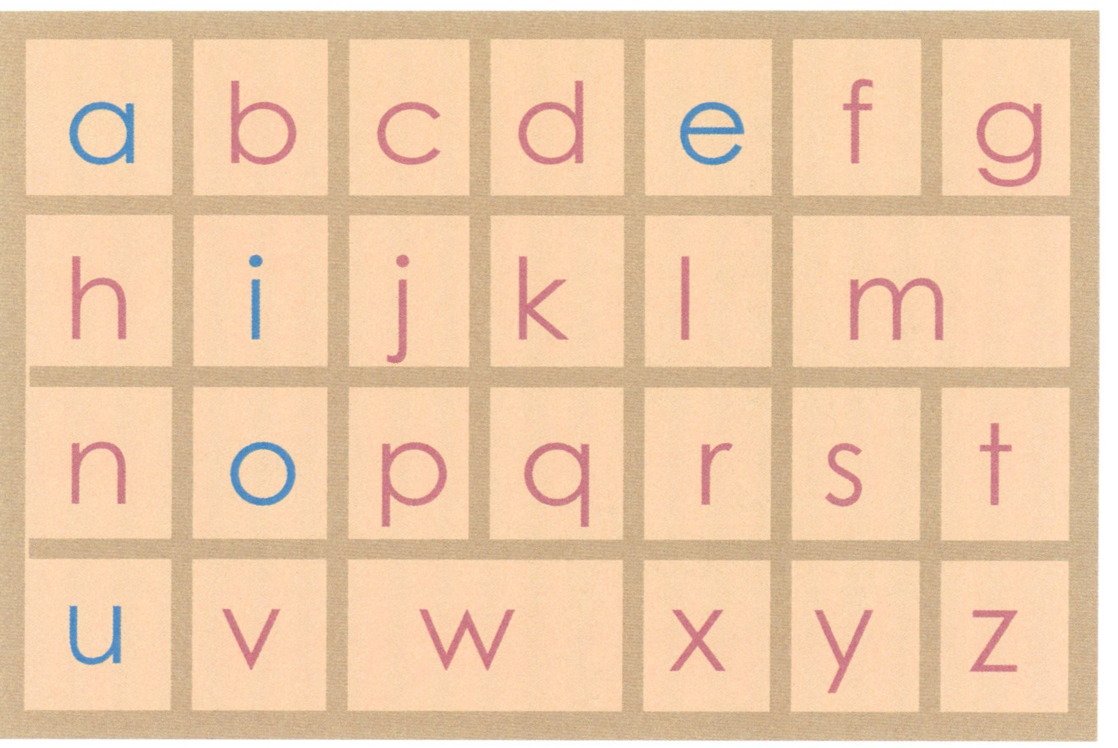
a b c d e f g
h i j k l m
n o p q r s t
u v w x y z

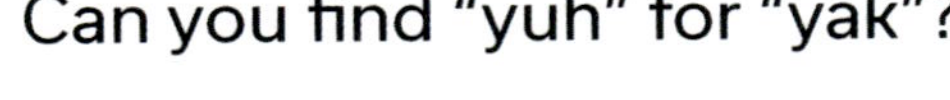
Can you find "yuh" for "yak"?

y

Say "yuh" for "yak."

Stop

In order to maintain your child's interest in the task and ability to continue learning, you will need to follow their pace. "Stop" pages are a reminder to offer your child a break, an extension lesson, or to continue on with the next lesson.

- Read Option A if you think it is time for a break, Option B if you are offering an extension writing lesson, or Option C if you are continuing.

- When you offer an extension lesson after a lesson, it's good practice to STOP for the day and start the next lesson another day. The extension lessons are only for children who can form letters.

- It is common for children to forget something they have just learned, so when you return, review the past lesson before starting the next one. Remember, it's a marathon, not a race.

A. You really stuck it out. Time to take a break.
I look forward to our next lesson together.
See you soon!
B. Nice work!
One more lesson before I go. Please get some paper. Now it's time to write your letters. Practice makes permanent.
C. Nice work!
Let's continue.

Lesson 3

Building Three-Letter Words

Tip

In this lesson, your child will learn that words have beginning, middle, and ending sounds. To isolate the difficulty of the lesson, we only offer one vowel at a time. The idea is for your child to have a good grasp of the middle-letter vowel sound and see the pattern of pink and blue, making it easier and more fun to learn. Help your child locate the letters if they can't find them easily. If your child struggles, emphasize the sound of the letter — for example, "ck-aaaah-/t/." The middle sound is usually the hardest for children to identify.

Repeat this lesson until it's easy for your child. Then, move to the next lesson.

Extension Lesson

Have your child copy the words they built and draw a picture to go with them. Then practice sounding them out.

Now you are ready to build three-letter words.
For this lesson, I will ask you for the beginning, middle, and ending letters to build a word.
When you point to the correct letter, the letter will be revealed.

How to do Lesson 3

Follow these steps and learn how:

Step 1: Cover the whole word on the right and read the dialogue for each letter.

Step 2: Slide your hand to reveal each letter after your child finds it (first the "c," then "a," then "t"). If your child struggles, help them find the letter.

Please say "try again" if your child chooses the incorrect letter. After two tries, help your child find the letter.

You and your child are now ready to start building three-letter words.

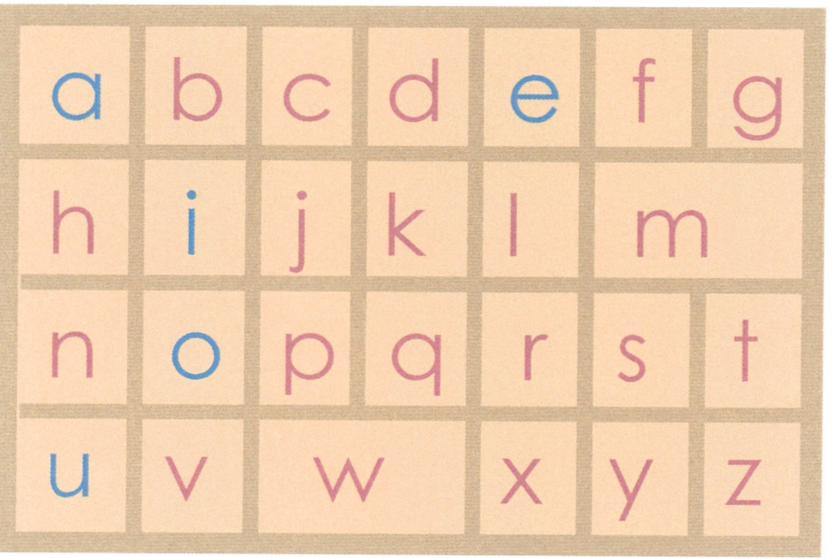

Can you find the beginning letter you hear in "**c**at"?

Can you find the middle letter you hear in "c**a**t"?

Can you find the ending letter you hear in "ca**t**"?

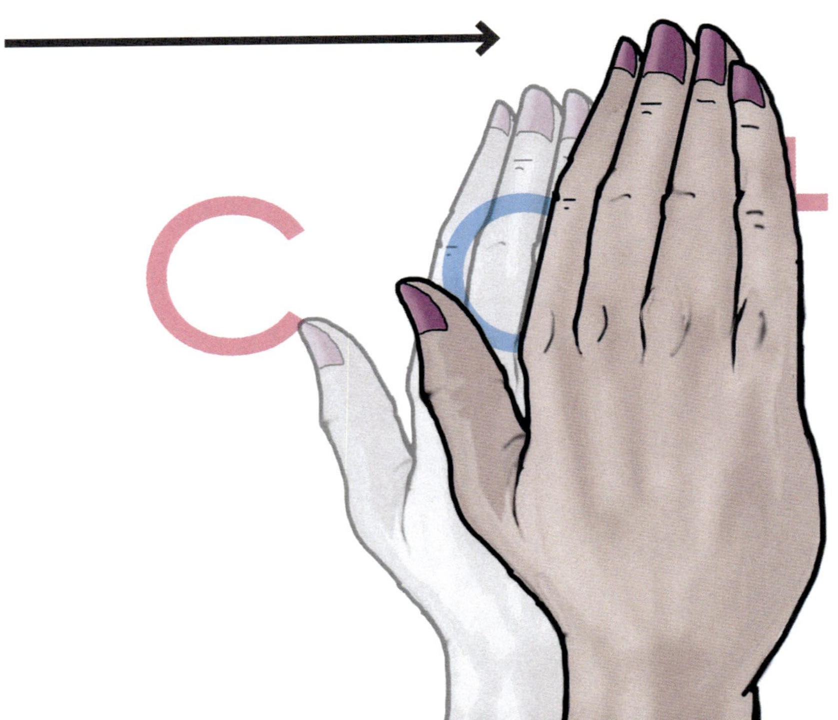

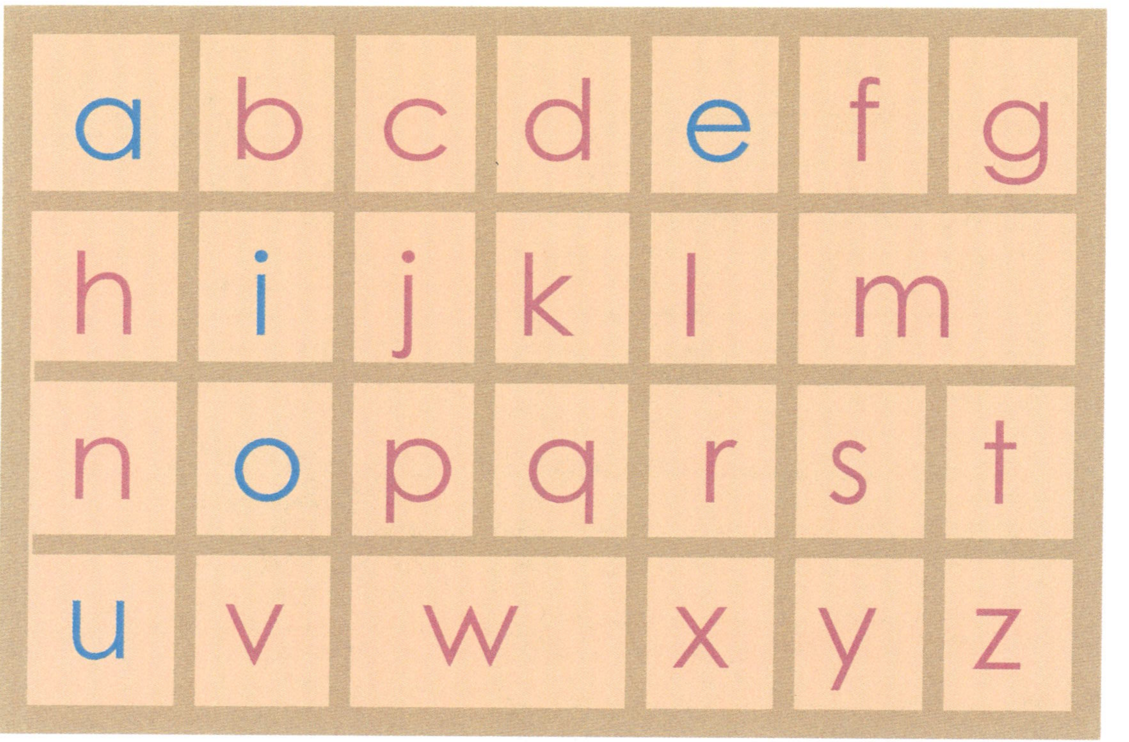
a b c d e f g
h i j k l m
n o p q r s t
u v w x y z

Can you find the beginning letter you hear in "**c**at"?

Can you find the middle letter you hear in "c**a**t"?

Can you find the ending letter you hear in "ca**t**"?

You built the word "ck-ah-/t/" which spells "cat"!

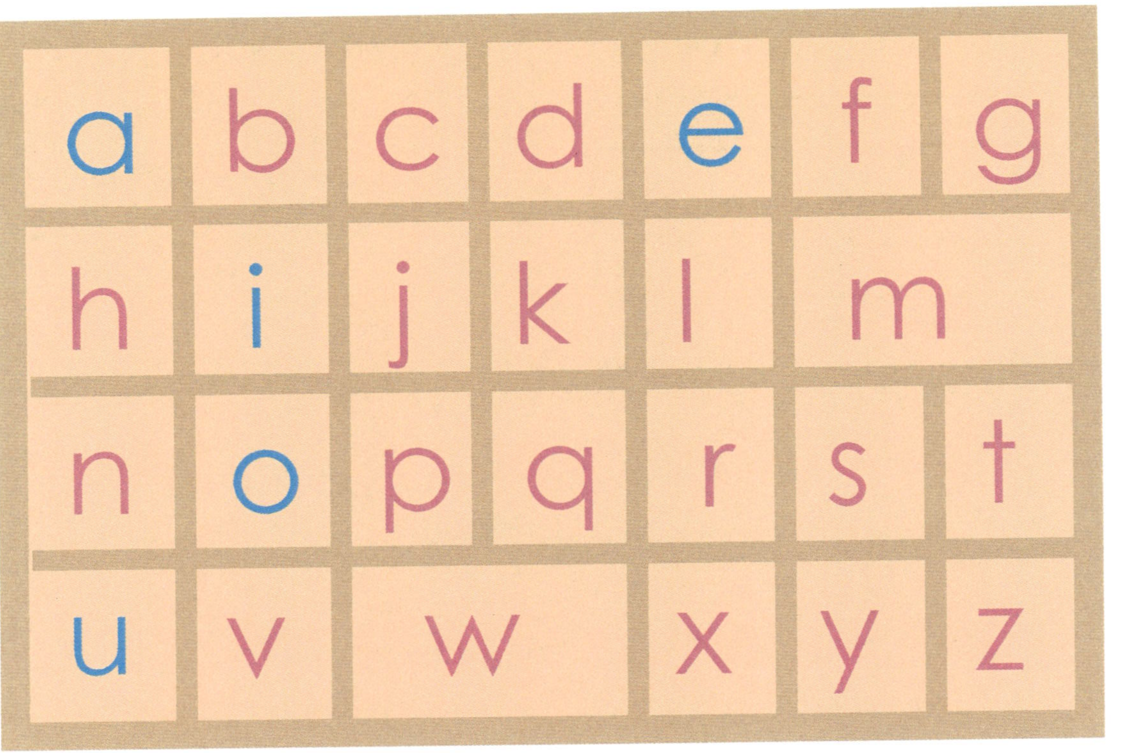
a b c d e f g
h i j k l m
n o p q r s t
u v w x y z

Can you find the beginning letter you hear in "**c**ap"?

Can you find the middle letter you hear in "c**a**p"?

Can you find the ending letter you hear in "ca**p**"?

You built the word "ck-ah-/p/" which spells "cap"!

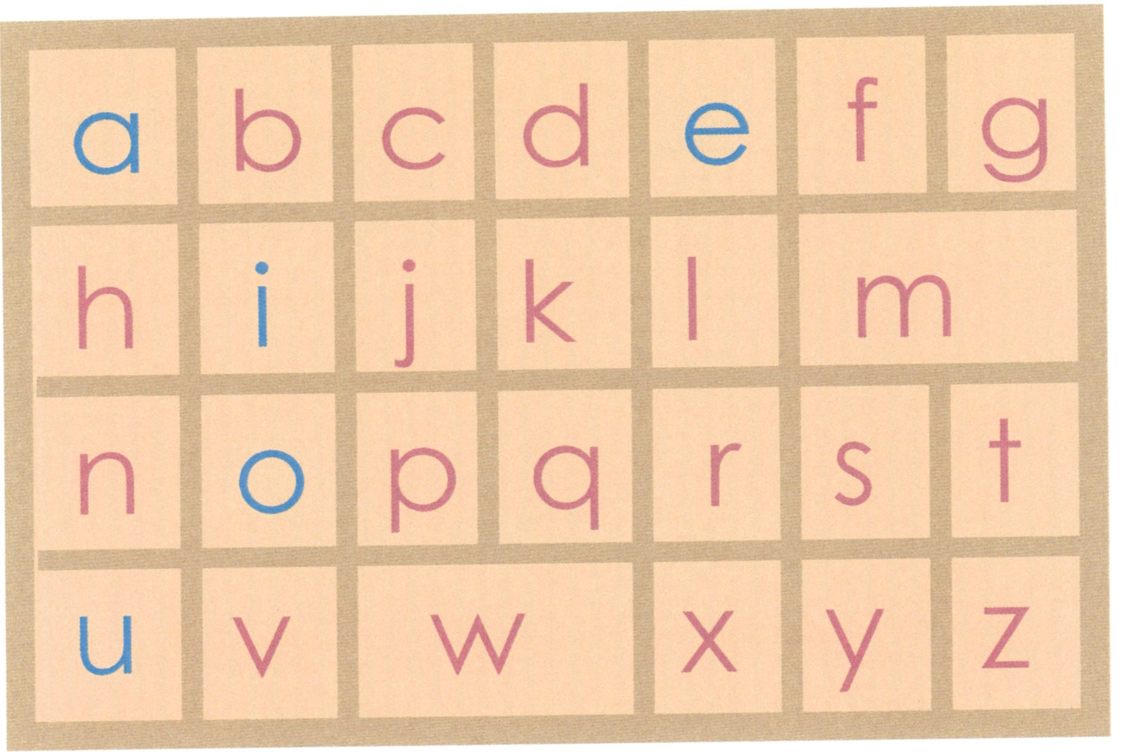
a b c d e f g
h i j k l m
n o p q r s t
u v w x y z

Can you find the beginning letter you hear in "**b**at"?

Can you find the middle letter you hear in "b**a**t"?

Can you find the ending letter you hear in "ba**t**"?

You built the word "buh-ah-/t/" which spells "bat"!

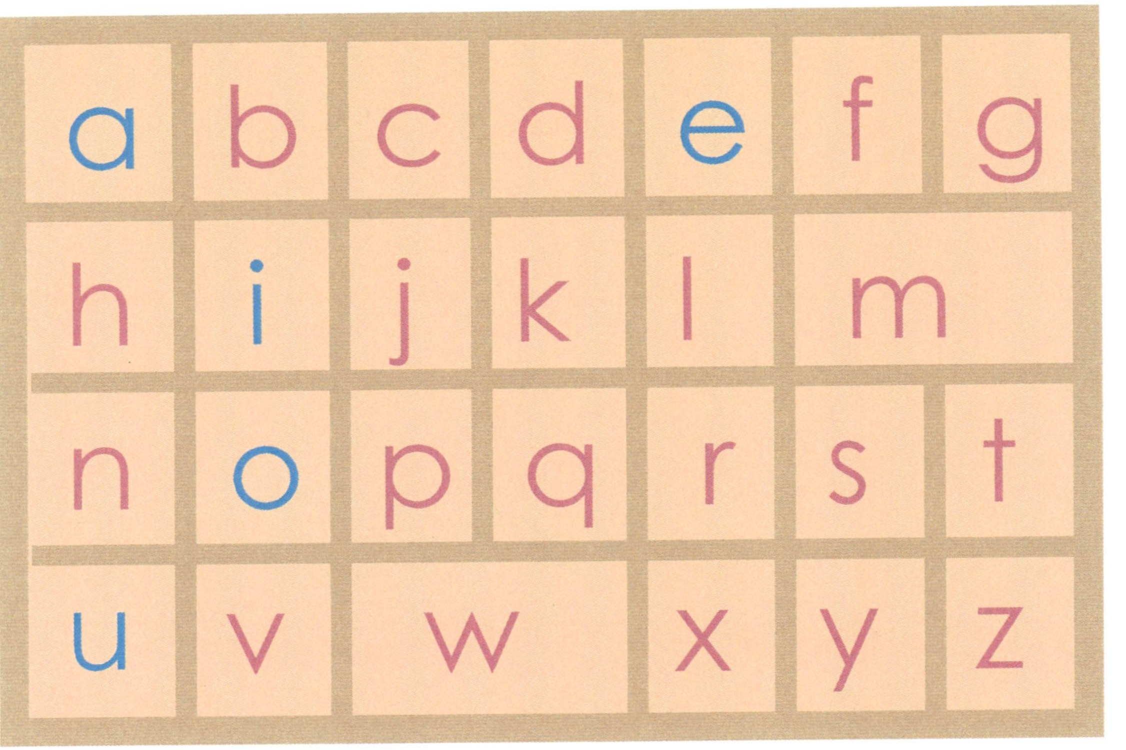
a b c d e f g
h i j k l m
n o p q r s t
u v w x y z

Can you find the beginning letter you hear in "**r**at"?

Can you find the middle letter you hear in "r**a**t"?

Can you find the ending letter you hear in "ra**t**"?

You built the word "Rrr-ah-/t/" which spells "rat"!

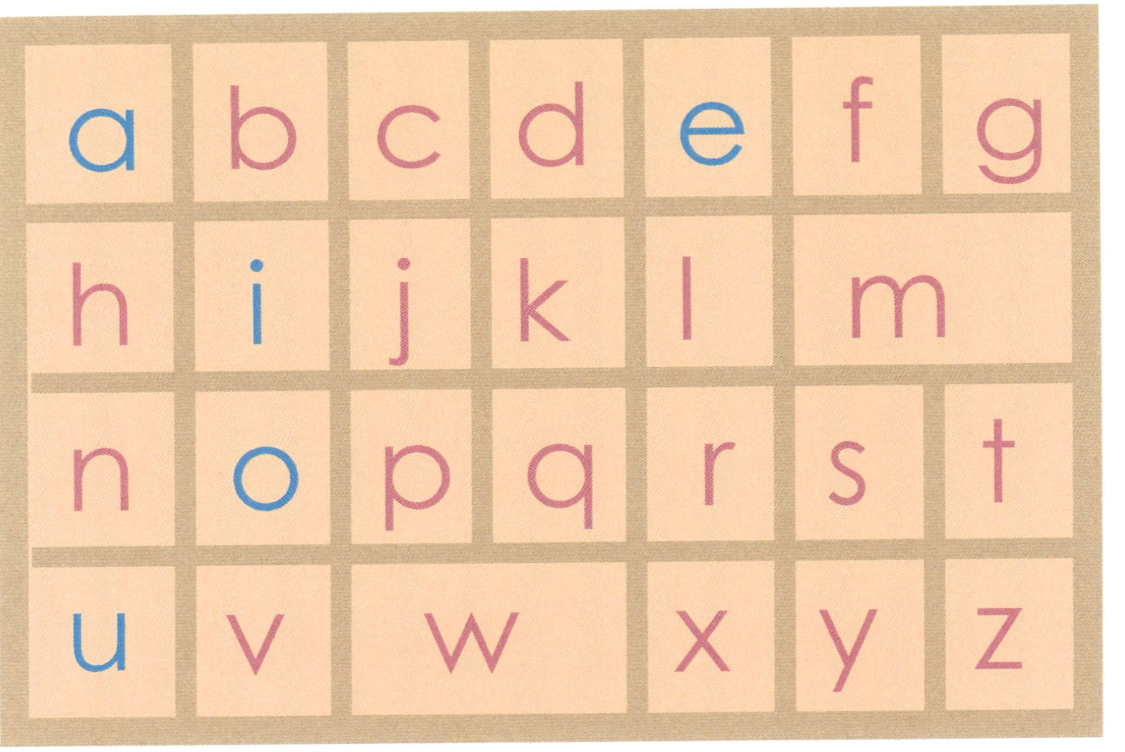
a b c d e f g
h i j k l m
n o p q r s t
u v w x y z

Can you find the beginning letter you hear in "**y**am"?

Can you find the middle letter you hear in "y**a**m"?

Can you find the ending letter you hear in "ya**m**"?

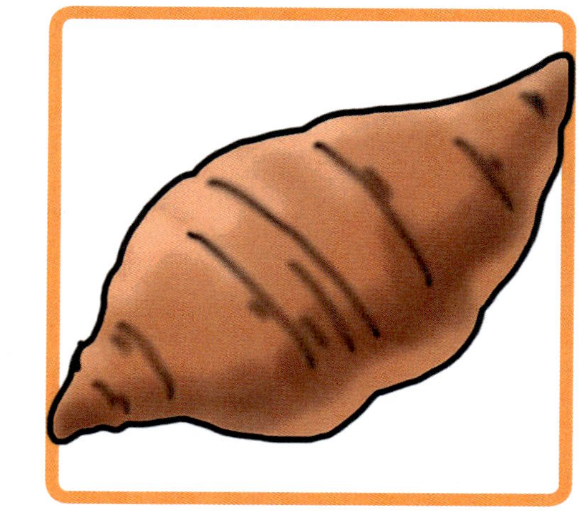

You built the word "yuh-ah-Mmm" which spells "yam"!

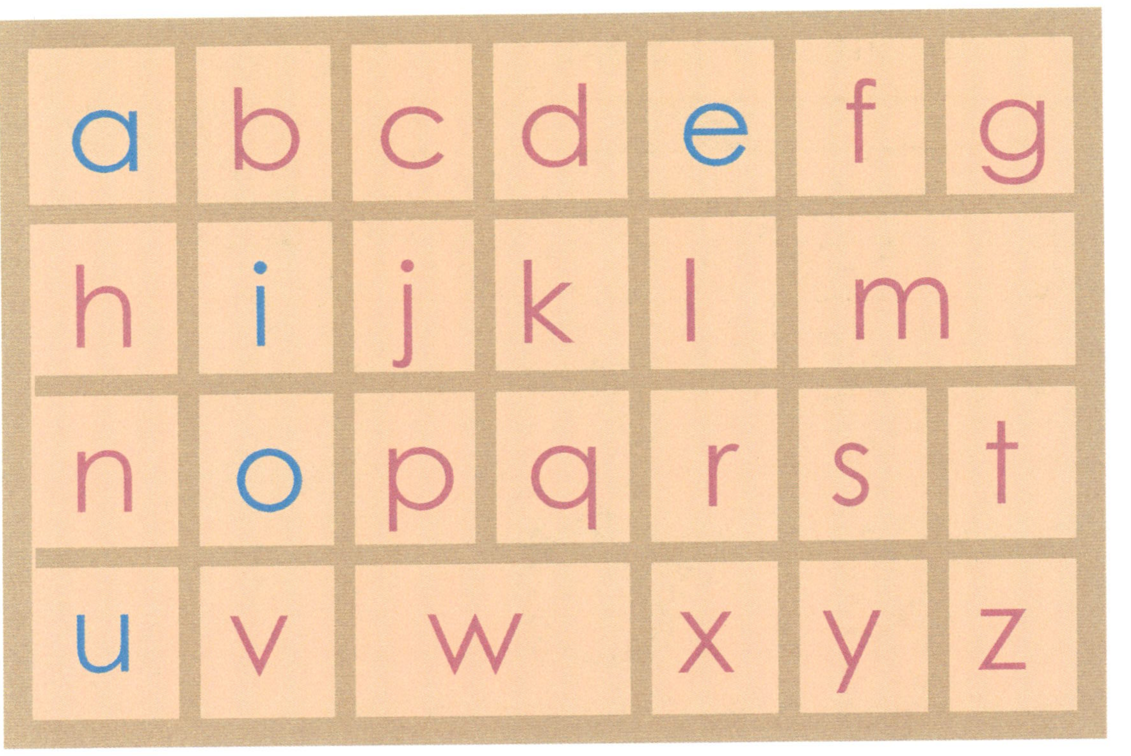
a b c d e f g
h i j k l m
n o p q r s t
u v w x y z

Can you find the beginning letter you hear in "**f**an"?

Can you find the middle letter you hear in "f**a**n"?

Can you find the ending letter you hear in "fa**n**"?

You built the word "Fff-ah-Nnn" which spells "fan"!

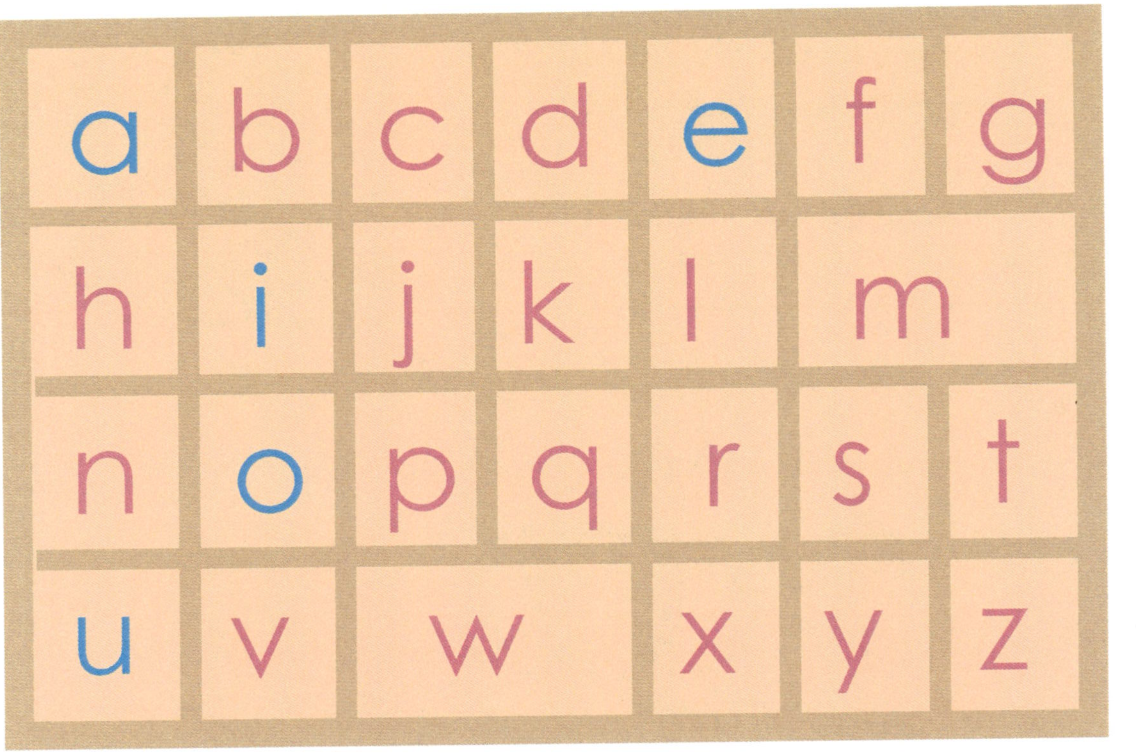
a b c d e f g
h i j k l m
n o p q r s t
u v w x y z

Can you find the beginning letter you hear in "**j**am"?

Can you find the middle letter you hear in "j**a**m"?

Can you find the ending letter you hear in "ja**m**"?

You built the word "juh-ah-Mmm" which spells "jam"!

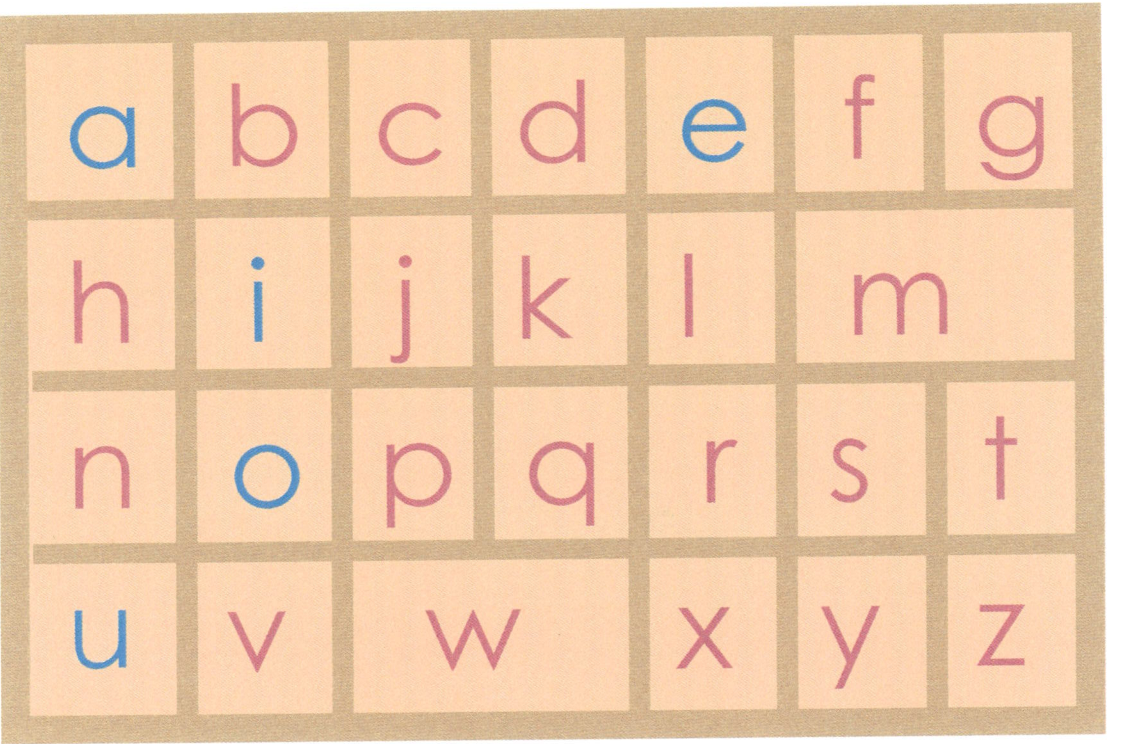
a b c d e f g
h i j k l m
n o p q r s t
u v w x y z

Can you find the beginning letter you hear in "**v**an"?

Can you find the middle letter you hear in "v**a**n"?

Can you find the ending letter you hear in "va**n**"?

You built the word "Vvv-ah-Nnn" which spells "van"!

A. You really stuck it out. Time to take a break.
I look forward to our next lesson together.
See you soon!
B. Nice work!
One more lesson before I go. Please get some paper. Now it's time to write your letters. Practice makes permanent.
C. Nice work!
Let's continue.

Lesson 4

Reading Three-Letter Words

Tip

This lesson bridges the gap from building a word to reading a word. Have your child place their finger under each letter as they read the word. As your child practices blending the letters together, they discover on their own that they can read. Some children learn very quickly and others need more practice for their brains to make the connection. If your child struggles, read the word with them and emphasize the sound of the letter — for example, "ck-aaaah-/t/, cat." Then, ask your child to try on their own. You will notice over time your child will pick up the pace as they discover they can read the words.

Extension Lesson

Have your child copy the words they built and read them back to you one more time.

Now you're ready to practice reading the words you built.
Let's get started!

The first word is "ck-aaaah-/t/, cat."
Now it's your turn.

cat
cap
rat
bat

The first word is "yuh-aaaaah-Mmm, yam."
Now it's your turn.

yam

jam

van

fan

The first word is "cat." Now read the words and find the matching picture.

cat

cap

rat

bat

The first word is "yam." Now read the words and find the matching picture.

yam

jam

van

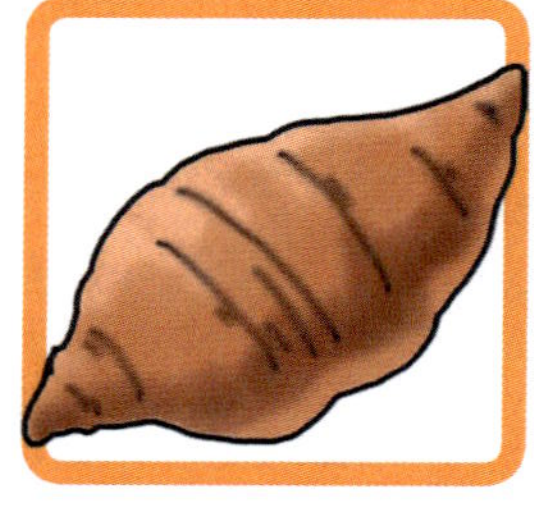

fan

Please read the words you built. Practice makes permanent!

cat yam

cap jam

rat van

bat fan

You completed your goal. Now, for one more game!

Just for fun, can you find the cat, three caps, and a fan?
Have fun looking! See you soon!

DO NOT TURN THIS PAGE
UNLESS YOUR CHILD HAS
MASTERED THIS BOOK.
a
a
ai
snail
abcdefg
hijklm
nopqrst
uvwxyz
rat
bat
mat
ca

Great Job!

Congratulations!
You reached your goal. You completed Orange Book 1. This golden cat is for you. Keep up the hard work, and I look forward to seeing you in the next book!

Accomplishments

The stamp is a symbol of your hard work. When you complete stamps for all the levels, you will be an advanced reader.

FAQ

How much time should I spend on the book?

- Daily repetition is the best way to learn new information. If you skip days, you may end up repeating past lessons.
- An ideal schedule would be at least five times a week for about 20 minutes per session.

Do I have to read the whole book?

- No. You can stop at the end of any lesson and restart at any time.
- You can also restart at any point in the book, depending on how well your child has grasped each lesson.

Is it okay to skip a section?

Yes. If your child has mastered a section, keep working on the other sections that are still challenging.

What should I do when my child completes a lesson?

FOLLOW THE CHILD—Ask your child if they would like to have another lesson. If they say "yes," continue. This indicates your child is still interested and enjoying their time with you.

When is my child ready for the next book?

In the back of this book are word lists you can review before advancing to the next book. When your child can read the words with ease, they are ready to advance to the next book. Remember, this is a marathon, not a race.

What are the core skills my child needs to learn to read?

- Decoding: sounding out words
- Vocabulary and comprehension of the English language
- Rules of the English language
- Memory and attention

Should I stop to explain when my child asks a question?

If your child has any questions about English-language rules, feel free to explain them as you go along. For example, "Mommy, why does the word 'rats' have an 's' at the end?" "Well, when there is more than one rat, you add an 's' at the end."

What is dyslexia?

Dyslexia is the most common reason children struggle when learning to read. It manifests differently for every child, and can range from mild to severe. At least ten percent of the population is dyslexic. This book is your tool to support your child; it is particularly effective in helping dyslexic children learn to read.

What should I do to build confidence in my child?

Review the last lesson your child worked on. Remind your child that with practice, you will find this new lesson is also easy. Give words of encouragement throughout the lessons. End the lesson anytime your child shows lack of readiness or interest. You can always revisit another time.

FAQ

What if my child is having trouble building the words?

When asking for a letter, always emphasize the sound of the letter you are asking for, such as "ck" for the first letter in "cat." This helps your child hear the individual sound in the word you want them to find.

What if my child is having trouble sounding out the words?

Reading is a multi-step skill and can be difficult for children to acquire. Beginning readers use one section of the brain to connect phonetic sounds to the letters. Later on, they use a second part of the brain to read words. It's a process that each child will go through and why children read very slowly at first. Then, a third part of the brain takes over and the child begins to recognize words. When this happens, the child can read much faster and begins to sight read.

What should I do if my child is having trouble focusing?

- TIME — Recognize your child may need breaks. Take a break after five minutes. Over time, slowly expand the time and the lesson.
- REPEAT — When you return, start at the beginning of the lesson. Each time your child will go further and further. When this lesson is easy, your child will be ready for the next challenge.

Review three letter "a" words

yam

jam

van

fan

cat

cap

rat

bat

New "a" words to read

hat

sap

can

dad

fat

lap

nap

sad

Made in the USA
Middletown, DE
18 March 2020